FRESH KILLS

CSU Poetry Series

LIII

FRESH KILLS
POEMS BY DAVID BRESKIN

Cleveland State University Poetry Center

ISBN 1-880834-31-6 (paper)
ISBN 1-880834-32-4 (cloth)

Library of Congress Catalog Number: 97-65397

First Edition

Published by the Cleveland State University Poetry Center
1983 East 24th Street, Cleveland, OH 44115-2440

Funded Through
Ohio Arts Council

727 East Main Street
Columbus, Ohio 43205-1796
(614) 466-2613

ACKNOWLEDGMENTS

My thanks are given to the editors of the following publications, where these poems first appeared:

ACM: "Fresh Kills," "Abort Retry Fail," "Slash and Burn," "Sendero Luminosa"

Alaska Quarterly Review: "A Small Boy, Your Son," "Youths Adrift in a New Germany Turn to Neo-Nazis"

B City: "Blues for Fatman," "The Unacceptable Lace of Capitalism"

Boatman's Quarterly Review: "Dark Canyon: A Brief History of the River"

Boulevard: "Turkey Baster"

Columbia Poetry Review: "Semtex / PA 103," "Documentary," "Lost Aisle of Dogs (Shopping Safeway)"

Denver Quarterly: "Jet Lag: Sometimes It Comes to This"

DoubleTake: "Watching the Grass Grow"

Fourteen Hills: "Pulse Points," "What the Shrink Told Us," "The Big One"

Harvard Magazine: "The Town Crier"

New American Writing: "Shatter Glass / Kristallnacht," "Smart Money," "Politics: No Stones No Fish No Wind," "Nothing on TV (Tonight)," "Da Hood," "Throw It Down (With Authority)"

The New Yorker: "Free Tibet," "Desk Work, After Hearing Bad News"

Nimrod: "The Winter Garden," "Christmas Quartet," "Valentine on 109th Street"

No Roses Review: "Chyna in the Land of Revolving Desserts"

The Paris Review: "Bugs," "Poem for a Businessman (Me)"

Poetry East: "A Divorce"

Press: "A Few Words for Our Unborn Child"

Salmagundi: "Rain for Nineteen Hours"

SEE: "Sunday Roundup"

Southern Poetry Review: "The Factory"

TriQuarterly: "The Day I Take Her to the Hospital," Evidence of Bear"

Western Humanities Review: "Chinese Airspace"

My gratitude as well to Fred Shafer for his careful reading of this work— encouragement, criticism, weakside help.

for Isabel
WITH LOVE

CONTENTS

THREE

ONE

POEM FOR A BUSINESSMAN (ME)

Sympathy, to begin with, is a problem.
The hotels are okay and there's free soap
to smuggle home. Lunches are not lavish
but good food mothers want their sons to eat.
There's pay. And hours. Vacations follow
seasons like soldiers in obedient
retreat. Plus the silent love of men
waiting for their bags at whirring airport
carousels. Someone says that stewardi
are hardly what they used to be. What is?
Sex is sex and politics, and speed has killed
the shoeshine boys. Eat fast or be eaten.

Being on hold is what hurts. Life stops
and static fills: fiber optic calls
so still my empty neurons firing echo.
For this fiscal my thinking is bearish
the man says. Projections get fired
like rockets or people. A real bear, I think,
would empty that office pretty quick, but
loading docks full of debt are fear enough.
First-in, first-out: FIFO. Last-in, first-out:
LIFO. Inventories stand in place like slaves
until they're laid, casually, by demand.
While I hold the line, spreadsheets wink at me.

Between the gates of night, domestic flights
from wives and kids I never had run counter
to the clock and land at lots of rental cars.
When I hit the lights, the windshield wipers
mock me. The parking brake unlocks the trunk.
A map displays my ignorance. Buying
everything in sight would solve some problems.
Jail would be a new one. Under rumbles
of descending jets the car-lot sentry
dances inside headphones. He checks my contract,
makes his mark and, smiling, hands it back.
The bottom line can't be read but shows my name.

BUGS

for Cynthia Moss

When humans watch the sky for holes, then kiss
all plants goodbye and suck down freeze-dried food
our ancient, desperate souls with pens ablaze
write debt-for-nature swaps like let's do lunch.

If gams are schools of whales but also legs
then maybe Moby's caught, her fishnet hose
so torn by drift net's yen for cash she bleeds
above the thigh, the moon blood red with coins.

If five of six animals are insect
and most of those are beetle, who are we
to save the world from orgies of the small?
One good bomb and they own the place, and cheap.

Wax and silk and pigment and honey: bugs
work so hard for us it's odd they sting
instead of strike. Butterflies near factories
turn black to hide from predators. Success.

Across the wobbly fist of earth, blue whales
are whispering to elephants: let's dance,
make love, burn swords of ivory and baleen,
stay up late, drink like there's no tomorrow.

Trekking in Tibet I meet the Dalai Lama.
Hello Dalai. Hello David. After some
hesitation and small talk, I ask him
what kind of washer/dryer combination
to buy. He says, "What is your universe
of choices?" Basically, it's down
to ASKO, the Swedish import, and Maytag,
the quality American product. The snow
contrail winging off Chomolungma turns
east toward Bhutan. A sign? I explain
that the ASKO duo is friendlier to all
living things—uses less electricity, water,
bleach, detergent—and gets clothes cleaner,
purples purpler, but costs twice as much.
The Maytag is spartan, righteous, renounces
superfluity, cleans okay, but throws repairmen
out of work. The Dalai Lama nods, sips
his yak butter tea and eyes a frisky dzo
in the yawn of Tingri Plains distance. I
consider his silence. Is this a reproach?
While waiting, and waiting, for his answer
I ponder *his* baggage: The Swedes had come
through with the Peace Prize, overdue, granted,
but still. Plus he's quite green, definitely
pro-planet. Is a dear object more material
than a cheap one? Would the *Buy American*
motive be dismissed as empty nationalism?
And yet who rides higher, astride his kiang,
with the banner of the nation-state, than he?
The huge head of Richard Gere, a tsonga blossom
in his hair, comes floating like a Macy's
Parade balloon above the snowcapped summit
of sacred Kailas. The Dalai Lama coughs,
reaches for a peppermint lozenge not yet
spoiled by the Chinese occupation, and says,
"Sometimes a belonging that doesn't work
properly creates suffering for us."

The pane of glass exploding like the sheets
of Klansmen riding like the ancient tailor freezing
wearing only bones like the hot metal fragging
the colonel's legs turning thighs to purple syrup:
a sheet of glass smashes into bullety bits.
The windshield, tempered and sloped to reduce
drag, like past drags on present, is the solution
to an engineering problem. Here's another:
how can the hidden roll bar deploy automatically
in an accident? Wheel-based electronic triggers.
The fake tube scientist says: These safety lessons
are too important not to share with our competition.

The same technology mechanism that parboiled
reduced simmered and reshaped Grandpa into a
lampshade now protects his moviemaking grandson
driving to the Beverly Hills Polo Lounge in his
black-on-black 322-horsepower 500SL with automatic
slip differential dual air bags and anti-locks.
Bumper sticker: I Brake For Fucking History.
These safety lessons are too important not to share.

With your shiny white bucks and wise stock
market selections, the finest crystal rings
at your wedding and lipstick smooches drip
champagne. At the Ritz-Carlton over Boston
Commons the Four Seasons over the Magnificent
Mile the Mandarin Oriental over the Golden
Gate or the Plaza over Central Park, the promise
of a happy bed and kitch comes with shattering
glass crushed by Florsheim wingtips. Kiss
the bride before imploding, then vacation
at a distance. The West Bank is lovely this time
of year. These safety lessons are too important.

RU-486, made by Roussel-Uclaf, may seem French,
and sister to Maalox, made by Rorer, which Rhône-
Poulenc controls, but in fact is mostly German,
since Hoechst controls Roussel-Uclaf, and in turn

owns Celanese in the States, not to be confused
with DuPont, which reminds us that without chemicals
life itself would be impossible. The big whopper
of advertising spreads the gospel of the brand

(I Like Ike, Be Like Mike) and brand identification
deepens into brand loyalty, which in a spreadsheet
resembles love. Does the cow love its brand?
Does the man saved by the roll bar love the brand
on his grandpa's arm in the old photo yellowing
like a fading star in the twilight attic? The dust
in that attic settles into termites, but the dust
in the shower has a half-life. Bury the buried.
Engineers suffer the shatter glass in vitro: a baby
bomb fragging device is as humane as it gets, or
would you prefer a coat hanger in the alley behind
the video store where Clarence Thomas rents sex tapes?

Backing over shatter glass when parking
is a trifling nuisance, like acacia spikes
to giraffe tongues, or stomach-crushing
baton blows to the TV news consumer. Never mind:
men in brown watched Disney flicks in the bunker.
Adolf liked ladies to shit on his head and so
he shat on us. Eva Braun could have been Madonna
if only the technology had been ready. These safety

lessons. In remembrance is the secret
of redemption. Get up in the morning slaving
for bread, sir, so that every mouth can be fed.
Progress goosesteps on. There is gentle glass
now that breaks into harmless rounded grains
instead of jagged shards. There is safety glass,
there is shatter glass. There is Bergen-Belsen
and there is Bergen, Norway. Never say
there is no hope. The eyes of Treblinka
are upon us. Never say it.

Bindlestiff with bonebreak skin and laptop,
batteries running low. The bilge water
of past crimes rises stanky. This fleapit

feeling won't last past dawn. Hiding below
the wall of mansions in raw red beard—a hank
for every anger—I fight each endless night

with the bitter blanket of fog. I'm an issue.
The neighbors show concern (with my hygiene)
and grow choleric re: litter. Trashed

inventory of expectations, binding energy
of failures rope me to my own cracked mast.
I'm hardly a molecule. What comfort in quarks?

If you cleaned the bacteria from my brain,
would I be less bioluminescent? The silver
handcuffs clink off for the last time, but

still stain. A rust of hours killed and schools
ticking like rotten pumpkins in snow. The small
thermonuclear device in my shirt pocket

is no Irish jig, no "Journey's End," or bingo
cry with me the winner, but is my shot
at getting clean, permanently, like the sun.

BIG CRINKLY

Unzippered speech of children,
shushed at school and museum,

competes with the can-opener
whine of the bright red Amigo,

battery-powered, rubber-wheeled,
designed for invalids. Like

this fat fuck, sagging, jowled,
sweating through the mall,

squinting and shopping, cursing
escalators and me, his impatient

two-bit summer stock son. Paying
with plastic all debts except

mine, all consuming, negotiating
the parking lot and arguing

our way back home, the perfect
Sunday finish. Will Copaxone

fix what beta interferons
promised but didn't? Napping

after a tin of Sara Lee
and Dr. Pepper, with myelin

sheath scraped and rotted,
from the inside out, he dreams.

BLUES FOR FATMAN

You. I sensed you in the sweet vulgar smell
of new Buicks, English Leather, and walls
of apartments just painted white, dying
for pictures, permanence, wives, or if you
were in a big bucks ripe mood to needle
me, fresh stains from a waterpistol fight.

Necessary nostalgia for your fight
now: locked into plastic chemical smell,
frowning and gray whale fat with a needle
punched into your dripping arm vein, the walls
of pale green ice and abstract prints leave you
sweating steel beads, snoring, but not dying.

MS won't slit your throat, but you're dying
to die, to lie still, unpained. The good fight
gone from your hollow spent bones, lazy you
drift through soap operas, sponge baths, the smell
of starched nurses, clocks, collapsible walls,
and that hissing silver getwell needle.

(Father: cortisone king junkie needle
armed dullfleshed man sexless hope dead dying
cold hospital crying blue in green walls
alone blue all blues got to got to fight
can't walk no wife no friends I know please smell
these pink pink roses opening for you.)

Sclerotic, chocolate smeared, checkbook poor you:
a baby in a big crib—the needle
pacifying cracked nerves which ooze and smell
like despair—whimpering but not dying,
whipping me, splitting me open (I fight
like mad) by closing your eyes into walls.

No shrink-wrapped wrecking ball could smash those walls
of rotten days and years, impacted you,
so thick with fear and regret. Too bad. Fight
now for my world of Sundays, dad. Needle
me witty and sharp till I'm so dying
with laughter I forget this bad scare smell.

I fight your slow sadness with no needle.
You stare hard into the hug of drugged walls.
I smell old doctors who can't see dying.

LOST AISLE OF DOGS (SHOPPING SAFEWAY)

Kill only things you understand, all else
let go. The maid spanks her lord like clockwork.
Bring me the sweat of Scottie Pippen, bankers
and brokers, meter maids. Analyze skin
for its content of wind. Excuse me, while
I kiss the skull. Birthing cows twitch like fish
on neon flies, the eddy circling backwards.
The kayak drills your stomach with its fist,
inside out Eskimo rolls the Klondike
caper. Eastern gods of yen buy Hawaii
not to mention Manhattan Kansas. Bulked
on steroids, yakuzas finger victims. Go slow.

Clip coupons. T-bills dogshit in rising
interest rate scenario but milkbones still
milkbones. Breath better, coat glowing, mind
sharp. The checkout girl has VPL and bags
under her armpits. Muzak makes the checks
go down like Darvon. Sting by strings, waltzing.

I'm no Martha, I'm no Vandella. Breast
tissue does not solve the problem. Pith helmets
dangle over Dopp kits, raised pleasure
dots packing. Don't jump to delusions here.
The countryside of ancient Rome combines
aqueducts with plastic pails, blue cranes, brown
flats: an eight-by-ten eye is big enough to
squeeze it. I'm falling apart here is what
Dustin says in the midnight hour, dobies
sniffing heels. Never help a victim. Go
seek help, wine or gun. A bullet in the nose
beats a quail in the bush, red foxes leaping.

PULSE POINTS

for I.T.B.

In dreams, your breasts are perfect and skin
thick fur against the cold of this distance.
What kind of fur? Prickly, matted, coarse, lux?
Jaguar black with hidden spots? I wait for you
to show yours. The tiger always attacks
from behind, so peasants in fields wear face
masks on the backs of their heads. Mine slips off
easy over chicken or the fine tilt
of your face. I invite attack. Blame me.

A snuck laugh about biceps or dreadlocks
is not an answer but a start. Someday
when I know you better, I will write you
a love poem, not this poem. Your big bold nose
will figure in, so too the vicious part
of your hair. Your eyes (with special notice
as to distance apart and radiance)
will have their place and the veined highway
of your forehead will predict the future.

In breasts, your dreams are perfect: the quick milk
of mother, lover, sister, nickname, love.
A foot on the floor at all times means trust.
Dogs sleep unknowing, but I know. You too.
Velcro, velvet, this tune goes to pulse points.
You said Basquiat paints planes, but in boxes:
freedom, power, movement, travel, soaring
stymied. You were right, but now you're pilot.
There's plenty of fuel and the ceiling's lifted.

Another planeload of baguettes leaves France.
Gay frogs leap into silk sheets and rivet.
The senator from South Carolina
reads a speech written on his fingernails
praising the values of tobacco leaves
while anchormen berate the obvious.
When I married you your lips were orange.
Blue sheep, blue sheep, blue sheep, blue sheep, blue sheep.
A hundred fuzz grazing in the Bhutan mist.
Fast food for the sneezing cold snow leopard.
This meal is broken, please fix it. Big cats
eat from the rump up. Small planes get fungus
in their fuel tanks, causing gauges to read
full when they're really empty. Nasty news.

POLITICS: NO STONES NO FISH NO WIND

Of course there's always a girl
in distress. But the trust
fund mistress, dead in her fire

engine red Porsche wearing
the senator's boxers, is not
on today's Beltway agenda.

The fleabag donkey leaps
up to bite the elephant's
wrinkled trunk and chokes

up barmy pesto of Sunday
pundits. Grizzle that V.P.
okay? Striped blueblood ties

boost his Q. For breakfast,
a hank of Republican platform
and skirl of Perot on morning

show. Don't be tetchy over
coffee. Which T-shirt to jog
in today? panders the candidate.

What medium message? Tumbleset
or somersault into the booth,
draw the wimple, spool your

grumpy tumid brain toward
the lever, tie a tumpline
to your expectations, and know

that you are being flensed
just as you yourself are trying
to flense the leviathan.

SMART MONEY

for Messrs. Segall, Gordon & Sweidan

Smart money swaggers into the room and eats
your lunch, then swivels and pauses, issuing
a belchless burp like Philip Morris
a smokeless cigarette, and devours
daintily the lunch of your friend. Smart

money has a meeting across the street under
another name. It was out of Arabians
and into Appaloosas before the horsey
set caught on. Reverse mortgage floaters
were appetizing eons ago, but now Russian

Vnesh ruble-denominated short-terms hedged
with Eurodollar options are spa cuisine
to a bulging balance sheet. Smart money
makes money going to the bathroom, hustles
through sleep to the morning's gold fix

croissant, keeps its receipts. Leveraging time
like a catapult cantilevers its stone, smart
money flings conviction at the margin
while scooping starfish from the tide pool's bounty.
It fired its lawyer while you paid yours up

the nose, it kissed off the girl that you kissed—
messy prenup to follow. It went long light sweet crude
when that seemed a tad insane. Smart money wiggles
into waders when there's blood in the streets,
sucking up the overflow to corner the transfusion

market in the next disaster. Smart money, callow
and refined, is short of course: the weather,
your future, DRAM chip makers (it's a commodity
stupid), the Shark at the Masters. Managed futures
provide a tale to wag the dog of debt. Smart money

only bites when the possibility of being bitten back
has regressed to the mean and is carrying the newspaper
in its mouth. Smart money knows the value of everything
and the price of nothing, standing on the dais, beaming
at its elder parents, out there somewhere in the gloom.

THE UNACCEPTABLE LACE OF CAPITALISM

Police Japan trying to curb unsavory trade.
Three businessmen vending machines sell
underwear "guaranteed worn by Japanese

The delicate waft of cherry

schoolgirl." $211,000 used panties sold.
Businessmen machines near primary schools
other meeting points young girls. $31

blossom tourist time plumps

per pair. Searching rule books police charged
entrepreneurs violating Antique Dealings Law
with needing dealer license. Used panties

the slow spinning silkworm

antiques? If underwear bought secondhand
yes. Also charged swindling if panties
not really worn young female students.

in its fine milky wallet

SUNDAY ROUNDUP

An eco-sensitive minimalist, he tagged his targets
on oversized Post-it notes. Cops could never make
the graffiti charge—willful defacing—stick.

Unison riffing must be accompanied by a skullcap.
The new F-16s carry *Fire-and-Forget* missiles, so pilots
can concentrate on their subsequent tasty targets.

My dog's on drugs. This morning she said to me,
A wedding is just like a funeral without the dead
body. Sick as a dog, a dust mop with legs, Daisy.

A pissed blue-collar stiff with a tourniquet tie
says on the talk show, She don't deserve welfare.
Baby sitters, jobs, he pustulates. Ninety percent

of all welfare recips are unmarried women. Frisky
matinees show nuns scowling at redheads and blondes
in spangled minis doing the frug while the boys

in the Coke-bottle glasses pony awkwardly. Fear
always has a reason. Upside down on El Capitan,
out of rope, capilene undies not wicking correctly,

synchilla pilling and day-glo booties glaring in mean
Sierra sun, for instance. A low buzz like fuzz face
in your amp, intermittent. A pipe bomb in your lingerie

catalog, at large among the end of summer specials.
The portly ex-coach buttons his vest against angioplasty,
clears his epiglottis, and returns to the color. No one

can deny a lot of life is poorly shot. The grizzled vet
with ruptured spleen and eye damage audibles at the line
of scrimmage while water-fetching Bolivian girls ask

for your help in lush but stark Sunday slick rags.
A cross word for the Contras is discouraged. Meanwhile
back on Wall Street, the expansionist CEO of American

Airlines vows never to buy another plane. So burned
he's currently in treatment. Whole mountains of debt
and no pitons except in stomachs on line at unemploy.

For the role of her boyfriend his chest got waxed. Men
come at you with rotating knives and sucking hoses
in the middle of REM sleep. Why not clean your grandma

with Q-tips and toothbrushes like they would a car
in Bel Air? God is in the detailing. Pinstripes
bleed like Red Wings gung ho for fisticuffs. Violence

shows the absence of power, quote unquote. Tell that
to the lady whose leg was brightly snipered yesterday.
The body song continues: those with bifocals fall

on escalators, Teddy Roosevelt liked to tap-dance,
a one-pound spool of spider web would unroll all the way
around the world. Some men only enjoy sex with breast

cancer victims and now there is a magazine especially
for them. The ads are Miesian. Not a cell in your body
was there seven years ago. The suggestion of change

is plausible. Even snoring can be cured with a simple
procedure: uvulopalatopharyngoplasty. The old party,
licking their right-wing mandate, warns that peace

is seductive but will just lead to war. Until Arafat
shaves, they won't believe it. In seven years, a whole
new snorting herd of cells. Same old, same old. Saxes

on vinyl cue the dark chemicals, which drop the velvet
curtain on the thrust stage, draw a warm and soapy bath
for the mind, and snuff the mirrored candles like hit men.

ABORT RETRY FAIL

for Fred Shafer

A suction of rotors squeezing
micron-thin particles

Erasure of emotion
to write again

The last man at the drugstore counter
when they stop serving the special forever

Unsold the idea sucks
all the blood out of the body

One vast peasantry planting
seeds in silicon

Falling forward toward
our expiration date

Mission-critical hardware
suffers in such conditions

Whether by retrorocket or retrovirus
the clock ticks backward

The last woman communicating
a disease: vengeance of the vanquished

TWO

THE BIG ONE

Will it cause the dead to dance?
They've been waiting, arrayed

around the sides of the room,
like so many wallflowers, fearful

foxtrotters, watching watching
fidgeting, sipping the dusty

punch, sizing up their options.
A quake might encourage them

to party, to at least adjust
their underwear, which after years

horizontal, has a tendency to
ride up. Or maybe husbands will

be thrown on top of wives after
years of side-by-side inaction

even when alive. And when they get
there, what? A coffin rub of wax

and wane? Ancient immigrants
who never cuddled, thrown into

spoons, disinherited grumbling
children with a chance to pound

some sense into musty parents,
and tiny tiny ones, whose birthdays

sent them out too weak for life,
eager, big-eyed, coming up for air.

SEMTEX / PA 103

in memoriam, David Dornstein (1963-1988)

10. My mother is weeping over my grave.
    She places a pink rose petal on my name.
    She kisses my name.
    The petal sticks to her lips for an instant.
    She washes the stone and the stone darkens.
    I see the stupidity of everything.

9. Tonight, on television, red water cascades from a fountain's
       crying mouth.
    Snow geese fly in circles above the site of the crash.
    Elvis makes good as a stock-car driver.

8. The point is to get from one place to another.
    All our lives, that's it.
    Squiggly tubes and tissue, ambitions, trivia, lunch boxes,
       clothing, desires, underwear, misunderstandings, all
       from one place to another.

7. I was a student of history.
    I see now even the stupidity of history.
    A revolution describes a perfect circle.
    Man is born free but everywhere is in chain stores.
    Those that don't know their fathers are condemned to be them.

6. I am now a student of SEMTEX.
    It has taught me everything again, in a brand new way.
    I bathe in SEMTEX, filling my bathtub with it, christening
       the hard yellow plastic rubber ducks of childhood.
    I eat SEMTEX, which is surprisingly tasty, especially with
       raspberries in the morning.
    SEMTEX is my pillow when I'm weary, my drink when I'm thirsty.
    It's my mail at noon and my love at night.
    Goodnight.

5. When I got to Scotland, the air was damp and cold, the men
       busy with shortwaves.
    I must say the investigators treated us very, very well.
    You'll get no complaints from me.

The entire bunch was first-rate, it was.
It was much worse for them than it was for us.
(Some of us still had shallowy breath, pulsing.)
The looks on their faces.

4. On Broadway at midnight, the bus driver exhales his last fare.
    He darkens his destination sign and nails pedal to floor.
    He wants to fly home.
    He thinks about his wife's fine fingernails in bed.
    He hasn't given me a thought.
    I'm not saying I'm hurt, but.

3. The florist's flowers bleed.
    The drunkard's ulcers bleed.
    The balance sheet bleeds.
    The boxer bleeds.
    The tape bleeds.
    The paint bleeds.
    The woman, she bleeds, baby.

2. Take one dumb horse's life, for instance.
    Standing so smooth and easy in the field, waiting for the stud,
        nibbling at Kentucky bluegrass under soft skies.
    Why is she not flying to battle, head erect and ears up?
    Why is she not under the Conquistador?
    The Confederate?
    The Roman?

1. We are all born dead.
    The early morning edition is dumped off the truck and swung
        onto the stand with the sad promise of tomorrow's head.
    A certain amount of living is done, somewhere between sea
        turtle and blue-footed booby.
    The woman inside the bank feeds the machines.
    The door of the past swings in, not out.
    My mother can't sleep, and she walks downstairs, and she turns
        on the set, and she takes her pill and she wets herself.

0.

NOSTALGIA

Riding the old train I used to ride when
I liked riding trains—past pouched loading docks,
scattering backyards, a fine mesh of trash
along the tracks—I watch the shadow-throwing
sun add heat to a past that felt cold
in its never-changing present. Dull tan
flutter of grounded leaves and skinless trees
bent by speed into Munch's clichéd screamers.
Lime and lemon and ice-blue houses hunch
proud, punched chins up, in March's slack frost.
A whitecapped beverage of my choice vibrates
on the tray. Cars at crossings wait, polite
as schoolbook stories. The small boy throwing
harmless rocks at us is me, unimproved,
in the gauzy warp of echo. It all feels
so toasty and hand-colored, so cordial:
how the gravel of my past becomes, under
pressure, under time, memory's diamond.

TROPICAL DEPRESSION

You're a real morning-after pill
is what she said. (A canceled flight
kept me there the night before.) Grim
business of approach, avoidance.
Someone had planted a small bomb
in her fuselage. Not my baby
I said. Well it's not just yours
is what she said. A fetus circling
nine months above O'Hare, waiting
for a landing slot. Ground control
to Major Mom, it's getting very hard.

In my dreams the pilot's Nixon
and we're going down. In the belly
button of the storm, the wind's skin
is soft and wet, but bending trees
snap like white trash husbands' tempers.
A palm is a palm is not true.
When its roots tear out, it's trash. Burn
it. Smell sulfur leaves twist inside
flames. Her morning-after breath
is a whole rich breakfast in bed
of discontent, expensive yellow
grief. Subway trains vacuum tunnels
clean with suction just by passing through.

The departure board gives a range
of flights, shuffles them with nervous
clicking and presents again: choose
yours. Tom over there, he drinks. Dick
screws around. Harry prefers nonstop
TV. This is a training film.
Observe the behavior of these
subjects. Does it crack a bell? When
I grab my flight, the stew's hip bumps
my head as she walks down the aisle
and the pilot's map displays each
couple in the path of the storm.

Formica fractures at this speed
of hate. Stay in the tub, hide, hold
your breath, breathe. By tomorrow's light,
she'll disperse and be downgraded
to a tropical depression.
Back to normal. Rain will fall more
slowly then, dirtying what's left.

A DIVORCE

Everything falls: Rome, leaves,
breasts, the apple, shadows across
the city of your good deeds.

The koala out of the tree,
grumpy drunk on eucalyptus,
is the dull ache of your teeth

after yesterday's drink, sleep
the only cure for life
and muscle-tearing dreams.

What is the name of the soft
knee she gave your groin? Who
owns your memory? Birds see seeds

from killing heights, free
fall with wings tucked then
trimmed, ready against need,

fall out of the sky without
caring, hatred, or kisses,
and land without looking back.

A SMALL BOY, YOUR SON

A few years back I taught him ball: the drop
step in the paint, the pick-and-roll, the base
line cut, how to keep his elbow in on free
throws, how to use his butt to shield the rock
from those who'd take it. In the sneakered squeak

of old wood floors and cold thumps of snowy
driveways, we played for fun and not for fun,
like anyone who cares. He was so small,
so slight, the peach fuzz on his arms so airy,
his milk mustache so comic and scary
I wondered would he ever grow? And when?

Now he's cutting classes and his wrists
with an exacto knife, knowing this will
kill you. (You'll *live*, which only makes it
worse.) Every time he shuts a door, he snaps
the whip of silence. His blank orbit grows

irregular. Experts say he's acting
out, or up, depending on their bias.
A slice of skin is quite an act you think:
where's his Oscar? In this small boy you've lost
the only prize your ex-wife gave you. Gifts
you gave come hurtling back broken but unused:

the electric guitar that could care less,
jumpless Air Jordans and wasted tickets
to the Bulls, Hendrix boxed sets, sundae treats,
explanations of divorce. He's weighed all
this and plowed it under. He knows how new

becomes old, how rust rots the teeth of marriage,
how the ground shakes beneath your feet. He knows
the appeal of an approaching train. Now,
on a drug beginning with the letter
Z, offspring of a certain compound P,
the doctors with their dosage plans can build

him back to being, but can't erase the scenes:
snarly sirens of police, I.V. drips
like grinding clocks, his squint against morning's
sullen light, a machinery of shrinks
stoking the bright furnace of hospital.

When we commit the boy to the clinic
we strip the parents of all illusions.
When we commit the boy to the clinic
we say to the parents *you must learn too.*
When we commit the boy newspaper ink
of all the world's stains comes off on your hands
and school will seem quite useless. Love never
felt so stupid, so dim as now. Driving
turns your car into a battering ram
if you're not careful, watch it. A backhoe
might attack you in the bathroom, brushing
your teeth with its claws. Breakfast won't be safe
and your job might scream like crazy homeless
people or your son. What I'm saying is
when we commit the boy to the clinic
expect these things and more. The sky will pour
a steady rain of hacksawed memories—
washed down gutters, sloshed to curbs, and sewered.
These forms you must fill out. And these. These too.

CRIB DEATH

The emptiness of accident
amid spastic clutter of clock

and phone is not a syndrome
or savory topic ripe

for family brunch, in-laws
creeping around with tea

on the careful carpet. Weather
steadies conversation, politics

seems safe, who do you like
in the Rose Bowl and how's work.

The virgin splatter of morning's
first light, after a wailing

sleepless night, shivers blue
through birches. A cold pinprick

sun rises in the west, backwards
in the bath mirror, like a wish

reversing memory into wish,
throwing light but no heat

on the standstill starry mobile
and the emptiness of accident.

PREGNANT

Up the slow river we walk like children
playing games. Thumb wrestling, singing badly.
In a lone canoe on a lake of ghosts
dead grandparents surface to take our bait.
The old chestnut mare, dogmeat in the field,
is not tender or picturesque. Just tired.

Rain falls, salting the scenery: roads turn
slick, buckled cabins drip, eucalyptus
trees take on the dull shine of sharkskin suits.
We could go inside or stay out freezing
but children have no choice. Where they're born, who
to, or why? They just are. New facts, born slaves.

Heading home, the car heater fails again
and again. Windows fog and our fingers
rub fast circles on the glass. We grieve more
for what we never had than what we lost.
An accident in the movies always
means a miscarriage, never a birth.

A FEW WORDS FOR OUR UNBORN CHILD

Comforting friends say there will be others
but you just missed tonight's voluptuous
sunset. Also the fat robin that flew
into the window today—falling stunned,
then flying away. The ongoing war
history books will ignore (too minor
to count in the grand sweep) won't even date
your birth. Glacial grind and deep treed forests
of Alaska continue breathing without you.
A white garbage truck comes and goes, its squeak
of air brakes and whine of compaction
the morning clock around here. Your diapers—
what they would have been—are not missed. You are

completely innocent of politics:
the suffocating flood of moral sweat
burst from the earthen dam, casually
ravaging towns named after religions.
Broken water mains and walls of coursing
mud the first culprits. Afterwards, disease.
To bring life into this death and disregard
for life is cocktail smalltalk for students
but we keep reaching for the tingly pippin
apple just above our heads. We asked you
and you said *Yes*: silent, clear, and almost
but not quite invisible. You didn't
tell us you were making other plans.

SOFT OPENING

Lemon flowers and lotus ponds, temples
on the corner, turndown service, chocolates:
these are the reasons I go away sad.
The ocean weaves a foam carpet and stars
watch sand pounded into butter frosting.
Castles drip from my hands like Dali clocks,
red ants march up the sun-blasted stucco
towing a dead bee. Rambutan, starfruit,
jackfruit, durian: as soon as I eat
I am asleep. The hotel soft opens
and I flit inside the happy cushioned
coffin of escape. The birds sing open
my mourning window and at night's first hint:
tokay, tokay, tokay, tokay, tokay,
tokay. The gecko speaks the simple truth.

TURKEY BASTER

My drive to his flight is filled with oldies
on the box, making me sad and happy
for a time I was not happy but liked
better than now. At the grim garage, I
pocket my parking stub and touch my breast
by accident. My heart ticks like the time
clock for the ticket my baby will be
some day, punching in late but arriving
safe. I've been behind a truck of worthless
men and could not pass for fear of loneliness.
Let's be honest: my heart's a canary
in yellow-bellied flight whose songs are cheap
but kind. I escalate into arrivals
where he'll walk through a gate numbered dumbly
with my age. The men will file up the ramp
with limp briefcases. I've seen this before.

While I wait, an enormous man goes down
clutching his left arm. A child screams and runs.
Orange jumpsuits come, glistening with hardware
and good intentions, triggering his feet
to jump as if he'd been tickled or scared.
But his body won't be tricked and stays dead.
His mind might still be racing or might be
nothing at all. A crowd gathers to watch
the dead man. We thank him with our presence
for his contribution to our lives. *Good
to be alive. Not me. There but for the grace.*
No matter, when my donor friend arrives,
I hope his scrotum hums with tiny fish.

BLACK DRESS

for Kim Bonnell

The black bow at the small of your back
is the long rope harpooned to your mother's
grave. You can't tie it yourself. Bad
cars sent you to a boarding school too young
to understand: the accident, her absence.
Now, childless and approaching forty,
driving sets you free, like death without
the memory of death. You always name
your cars. They take you away smoothly.

Tonight, your naked back feels cubist
and daggers down your legs make cocktail
chatter hateful. The black tie affair is
the only one you'll have now, although
your shiny dress alone could mark a trail
for treasure. Marriage is a gold mine
of work. Children mean serious business.
The season of the little black dress never
ends and diapers do not constitute a look.

Driving into country, road smells drop into
your dark car like recipe ingredients:
pine cone, diesel, willow, dead skunk, river.
You drive for antiques but dream this instead:
at a dirt road diner, you sit alone
at a booth for six, eating scrambled eggs
out of a bird's nest on your plate. Then
you walk into a field of bright grass, lie
down, touch yourself, and give birth laughing.

PILLOW TALK

Your brain can only be as big as my
vagina croons mom to son, cradling head
on belly, swooning like a torch singer
in the extravagant flicker of two
a.m. This fact, though true, will come to haunt
the boy for the rest of his upright life.

Brain first he bawled into the world, and brain
last he'll meet his makers on junior high
trysts, in dorms and coupes, alleys, cathouses,
movies, rec rooms, on wrestling mats of shag
carpet, blowing beaches, wet summer lawns.
Brain size leveled off a hundred thousand

years ago. At birth a swollen quarter
of its final bulk (while the remaining
body weighs in at a puny twentieth)
a bigger noodle just won't make it through
the demure pelvis. At least this accounts
for the vast number of Republicans

scouring our states, squinting, dim, beaveresque
in their excited ardor for chopping
up the landscape into edible chips
to be wolfed down with mild salsa
while watching Monday Night mayhem.
Hedgehogging bets with private schools and tax

cuts—cut the feed, cut the feed from Congress
on this pubic access channel, reinstate
domestic hiss: Mom rocks baby to Bach
and Aretha, wondering how this little
monster squiggled out of her. She coos
Your brain's bigger than daddy but not me.

CHYNA IN THE LAND OF REVOLVING DESSERTS

for Chyna Darby

Jaguars jump with the grace she pours malts.
What's extra in the silver vessel is key.
Something for nothing, a bright surface

cynicism. Let's make some sense of this:
She's dancing fast but not the two-step,
kneedeep in french fries and recovery
at the fake diner. Her tattoo is blue and

she has tambourine eyes. You can see the veins
in her forehead. Has she ever shot up? Is
she fixed, like her thirteen cats? Me-*ow*.

Cranberries give apple pie a certain blood-
shot morning-after vibe. Her motor scooter
spews all smoke not trapped in her lungs.
Smokey sings "Mickey's Monkey" on the juke.

The heavy southern atmosphere, a humid
ripeness best expressed by paired guitars
drunk with reverb and wah or perhaps by

Chyna's interstitial thigh under job-related
chinos, not to mention a certain need
for the anti-pain in high school and hateful
immediate ancestors, is why she escaped Atlanta

and ended on a Sausalito houseboat, sniffing
mildewed businessmen with money and gay times.
Lesbians lick their wounds and go about

their business. Silence sometimes does not
equal death, but in fact is a pleasant reprieve
from the tinny shouting of everyone's need to be
special. Life is more than just upside down pink

triangles. The Marlboro Man, unpierced, rides herd
at the AA meetings—caffeine is doled like methadone,
cigs get nervously sucked, slips are appraised.

And she thought consumption was a nineteenth century
illness. The ashram in India will make her throw
everything out: books, clothes, jewelry, cats, vans.
The walk-in closet in her head is more of a problem.

is the day she needs me to help her move
into her seventh apartment of the decade.
What a male partner did or didn't do to her

at the firm has sent her over the cliff
she's always driven close to the edge
of, thick wind in her blonde piled tangles,

skinned knees from bumping into things,
paranoia. I've grown accustomed to your mace
is what I say when her purse spills open

and deltas everything onto the stained
rug. We make three sweaty trips, stuffing
my car to its gills, poking through the sun

roof. Her glassy eyes and quivering bottom
lip suggest restrained fear but her closets
cry hysterical: hand-me-downs of sister

and neverworn pouffy dresses of mom, old
crinkled plastic bags of golf balls and tees
(two lessons four years ago), thirty-three

pairs of shoes (two of the steep red fuck-me
variety), brown garbage bags full of old
blouses, modems, small unmarked samples

from famous bodies (the Colorado, the Coruh,
the Urumbamba, the Alsek, the Antarctic Sea)
in antique bottles with chipped stoppers,

ultra-slim feminine hygiene products, dog-eared
gifts I gave her. She shows me a huge potato
shaped like a heart she's been secretly saving

in the fridge. Her collected Shakespeare,
turned to a favorite sonnet regarding love
and its surprising consequence, splays

facedown on the bed. Rabbit ears spring
from the unwatched TV. Sitting on the crusty
kitchen stove, a wicker basket of legal briefs

and arcane judicial rulings on environmental
issues—which, when extrapolated geometrically
will save the planet, she hopes. Her upside down

bicycle rides the bathtub, honeysuckle body
oil coating the handlebars. I walk the bike
to her new apartment while she showers, packs

and angers herself anew over her firm's posture
re: the harassment charge. When I drive her
to the hospital, we hold hands in the useless way

we used to. Upon first look, we're not pleased
by the place: no porch, ponds or grounds. No
swans. The attendants loom invisible behind

large bushes and blank brown brick walls.
A single woman stands in the parking lot
smoking, windmilling her arms to the command

of the private fitness expert in her head.
We swerve away for a last ice cream—soft serve,
chocolate dipped. The frozen chocolate cracks

off her cone when she licks it. One tongue
lunge and she's saved a bit but spoiled her face.
Heat, tears, ice cream, trembling: her makeup

gets a mad clown look, like the self-portrait
she painted in first grade and left in my trunk
after moving today. As we drive slowly back

to the hospital, I clean her mouth's corners
with an index finger of my spit. We park
and sit in the blasting sun, criticizing

the lack of swans. I walk her baggage in
and hug her goodbye just as the clipboards
come marching down the hall to get her.

VALENTINE ON 109TH STREET

The memory of bean soup to the man
shaking on the supermarket grating.
Or the stream of blue buses in icy
fluorescent glare, exhausted and empty
on Broadway at night. Why not the ticket
taker in her glass cage, lipstick trembling
around a cigarette of fives and tens?
Any cliché will do for me now, asleep
at the wheel of my life, drugged by the cure
that is the disease, on the hazy couch,
saying prayers for Wilby's Bar & Grill, torn
down for condos, prayers for all small buildings
imploded and replaced, for all people
on the bayonet-end of elections
in those tired countries the news does not want
to understand. Leap

                of faith. If I fell
off the couch, a sliver of floor might pierce
my forehead and change my channels for good.
I ponder the resiliency of foam,
the life expectancy of an old stained
Turkish carpet, the steady spray of cathode
ray. I have produced nothing to consume
for more weeks of this winter than I care
to count. Such ethics blur into distant
maps of intrigue and escape. This feeling
of hollow, of lonely marrow and wounded
tongue, is not the only goddamn reason
for a valentine, but there is no better,
when she comes to me, eager in her bones,
holding up the day with her soft, large hands.

CHRISTMAS QUARTET

1.   The Crash

When all the leaves fall from the banks
and lashing rains like cold tongues wipe
the streets from fail, I listen to news
of a worse world and losses mounting.
There is only so much that can be done.
The towns of our grandfathers, fired
in mud and quick with ideas, come tumbling
back into headlines of insurance fraud
and movie scandal.

                    There are tractors on farms
that will stop now, and buildings that won't
or will come down, all depending, let's see,
on the choices of the private sector. Crowds
huddle on the corner awaiting next morning's
news, soaked by the passing bus splash
of Tokyo or rusting towns of Great Lakes
where industrial parks won't go. Didn't
you always trust her? Didn't she give you
her word and say this wouldn't be so?
The digits move and the alarm still rings
but the bed is empty in your eyes
of the future.

2.   Lonely Woman

On Columbus before it gets rich,
I pass facades full of beer and stray parts
for old cars by Marvin Gaye Garden. Bleeding
steam, the street's been cut by the blade
that got me last month. A young woman
screams, "I don't have it," into a corner
pay phone, rocking back and forth in the cold.
Then she listens, tears drying white
in the wind. She fists the plexiglass

and shouts, "Look, I don't have a home
and I got three kids in the car and I don't
have it." When she slams down the phone,
it falls and hangs,
                    dangling and twisted.
She hurries to her car, puffing gray exhaust,
parked illegal, three kids in back, two
of them strapped squirming in baby seats.
Shame is too easy for what I feel, agreeing
with her, united in falling apart. The car's
an old taxi, fading and unmarked. When she
throws it into drive, it seizes and stalls,
as the lights turn red, one after another.

3.   Lookout for Hope

Clouds uncertain of their futures
are what I find at the bar tonight.
Perry and Danny do their Irish routine
for the regulars. With the holidays so close
waitresses stop dreaming of auditions
and sweep tips off tables like toll collectors.
Both TVs show sports, one college football
and one the nighttime sulkies. No one
cares. We settle for the vague abstract glow
and thank the gods for heat.

                            The sound
of the bottle as it doesn't smash against
the glass window is what I feel tonight.
The ash in the tray, the jukebox that doesn't
play and isn't here, is what I feel. Young men
in Polo sweaters insult their girlfriends
and everybody laughs. It doesn't have to be
this way and the world has half a chance
is what I say to no one. I drink what's left
and refuse all offers, thinking hope travels
faster than the speed of light and slower
even slower than time.

4.   To Drop at the Cry of a Hat

At the scratch of your keys on my door,
thrown in anger, or the way you touch
your head when it hurts, under my eyelids
at night you dance so splendidly still,
in the ache of the sun slipping down,
and morning cold so metal it hurts,
to the turn of your body on the street,
dancing away again and waving hello
is goodbye, to opera in bed and the crumbs
of divorce, for the part of you I could
not touch and

                    the part of you I touched,
for the horses that want your ride or legs,
and the boys in their line expecting a turn,
in the dull of the night when the phone
rings once and not again, in the fall
from grace that makes me stand, still,
at the thought of a number, an awning,
a walk up the stairs to a sticky lock
that always opened, comes the beat
of my eyes in the cry of my life,
alone, and disappearing.

LOST AND FOUND IN NEW HAVEN

The vodka-cut artery spurts blood
into the brain. Seven headless women
dance, a daydream of old lovers training
to see Emily, the sweetbreathed baby
born to the old best friend. We all have names
others give us. There there child, sleep now,
sweet dreams, I imagine saying. All the atoms
rest tonight: uranium, plutonium,
beryllium, tritium—water as heavy
as heartbreak. It is the first day of spring
and somehow snowing,

                     every flake floating
to its death on the mingy ground. Ancient
acid-veined stones streak the right of way.
Garbage too, used shoes, weeds, industrial
rags, fraying closed tool shops. Gray train yards
in sleet wet and bone cold hiss my arrival.
No matter what the mayor says this town
has had it. The old station, pumped full
of money, smiles with new paint and gilding,
like the patient on narcotics in intensive
care. Here, the trains still come and go in both
directions but always end up

                 where they start.
Outside the station, dogs chase each other
in circles. The flat matted grass, frosted
lime and mud, tears away in clumps. Ducks paddle
under the highway. A gauzy red canvas
up against a concrete wall is the scene
of the crime: automatic weapons spray,
a pool bottom draining, a holey chest,
nothing at all. I seem to have misplaced
my future wife. Every night the morning
comes too fast, off its tracks and grinding.

THE SPONGE

Like a boy on his first flight
asking to see the cockpit
I look into the machinery
of her moans and blow dust
off the smooth surfaces.

The technology of love is
no empty gesture. Seabirds
have bones full of air, for lift,
and yet the wandering albatross
needs wind to fly. On calm days

it can only sit on the ocean,
humming. Plus, a certain
anemone has a mouth that doubles
as an anus. That would make
it a shock-jock with good

ratings. The wombat and pygmy
hippo mate casually but
without ulterior motives.
Alcantara is a miracle fabric
that can lead to breeding

if used smartly on bed frames.
Where rivers debouch into
seas, penguins slip into
balmy cauldrons. Some females
can manufacture fertile eggs

without mating. Send in
the clones. Don't worry, she's
here: my parthenogenetic
insignificant other. Not
to mention the sea horse

would be a mistake, or
the frog who gives birth
through *his* mouth. Who needs
a spine when you can be a
nudibranch? Small talk is

functional. When you mash
the tissue of a sponge through
cloth, the resulting inchoate
broth will reassemble as a new
organism. So she may turn

tricks or do deals, wipe tears
and makeup off, change clothes
(veils, mirrors, slips, colors)
and become again herself,
a new song not yet on the radio.

DESK WORK, AFTER HEARING BAD NEWS

for Chelsea Hadley

I could use the stapler to staple
my eyes shut. That hurt would help

me cope with the sunlit young woman,
bursting at her seams, her angel

face wrecked in an accident
prompted by a party. The squeal

before the thud, the squeal before
the thud is all she remembers

in these early days of after.
Is her loss just surface or something

deeper? The mirror sets the table
for the rest of our lives, but others

see us more than we will ever see
ourselves. Tonight, we dine on shards.

SLASH AND BURN

Say you're wild dog or sleepy cheetah
kissed by sun through smoke, flushed tumbling
out of womb with afterbirth a sauce on dirt.
Is fear just a quint without mother's milk?
The others, scrambling for nipples, yapping
eyeless desires in baobab heaven.

Today my model friend's in Paris, France.
In grand hotel, she reads the morning news.
They're digging out her window and she smokes.
The subject of her story, Health Physics:
to push the outside of the envelope
of what a body can take—rems, heat, half-
lives, ultra-violent rays. And bellboys see
her body is the envelope, licked.

Way up the Golden Triangle, Mekong
villagers fry snakes in crispy wind
unleashed by sweet soft green wood, blackening
ground for fast-food crops, for cash, and killing
all but insects. A wise man, though, can burn
paper with current coursing through his skin.

Maybe in Brazil, lifting groins of earth
for gold, the peons kiss their luck. But men
with guns for whips don't suck the barrels dry.
They know who's boss. Whose back breaks the ticking
of the owner's clock. Whose woozy wife knocks
back gin, and holds it like a worm in beak
for her little nestling's supper. Splendid
excavations for such precious metals sing.

Say you're me. Overwrought. In Chicago.
And you're splitting matter with a loved one,
slamming doors on teeth and pulling hair
of past disputes. You think: the vicious kiss
of desire, acquisition. Leasing space
in your heart, abandoning the building.

THREE

DA HOOD

Hitler, Pippen, Barkley, Shakespeare, Payton.
Gromyko, Nintendo, Kaifu, Hitler.
Boesky, Milken, Hitler, Icahn, Buffett.
Ellington, Armstrong, Monk, Hitler, Mingus.
Teller, Hitler, Oppenheimer, Spielberg.

Mother, father, Hitler, brother, daughter.
Hitler, marble, granite, sandstone, concrete.
River, ocean, isthmus, Hitler, glacier.
Grass, trees, sky, dirt, field, playground, cave, Hitler.
Diamond, apartheid, Hitler, Sendero.

Castro, Mitterand, Thatcher, Hitler, Quayle.
Springsteen, Hitler, Prince, Bono, Nicholson.
Weegee, Winogrand, Frank, Cosby, Hitler.
Gehry, Meier, Hitler, van der Rohe, Graves.
Dolphin, Monkey, Bat, Snake, Fly, Elephant.

DOCUMENTARY

Blue cranes among kudu,
the sand grouse captured
by terrapin teeth, a black
crane standing on the nose
of a rhino, pecking at the
bright red gash where the
horn's been ripped off in
a battle for sex.

Rubber bustier, high heels
tweak the unpainted ass, rouge
nipples plus Angel Cordero's
riding crop is the contrasty
mise en scene, the Malibu beach
house, rented by the hour to
feed the frenzy of Hitchcock
sharks, Peckinpah bloody lips,
parted, licky teeth.

Ostrich by zebra by springbok,
the banded mongooses rile warthogs
and blacksmith plovers, while
the snorkeling python, nostrils
hidden in the water weed, goes at
the Egyptian goose, which flies,
but the red-billed coot is not
so lucky. Flamingos are rarely
seen with wildebeest.

Lace teddy, police nightstick,
Uma Thurmanish, soft focus,
flexible muted cries on formica,
local three-piece suit unzipped,
certain kinds of fellas squeezing
those two dimples above her hind
quarters, smiling purse, certainly
exchange of bills.

Avocet sweep the cloudy water
with bills for small change of
crustaceans. Another Kennedy
drives off another bridge.
The jackal makes everyone

at the water hole slightly
apprehensive. Hot tubs are
traditional for this kind of
shot, where she's on top.
Everyone is making a living.

WATCHING THE GRASS GROW

for The Big Man

Even Nat King Cole, so smooth
he became white in the eyes
of many, had his lawn manicured

to the tune of *NIGGER*
in the city where the angels
stay lost. His daughter Cookie

saw the mark and sobbed
all the way to school, her fancy
house and famous dad meaning

nothing suddenly. The grass
grew back so slowly, the shadow
of the long-burned word echoed

acrid on that lawn for months.
In the rich dark dirt it sounds
still: black, unforgettable.

MILES DAVIS

Funk so deep you were half the time
drowning: pretzeling your fingers
for Irving Penn, shooting the bird

to Ferrari-chasing heat, rope-
tying women who only *thought*
they were in love with you. Swimming

with your fists clenched, you swallowed
bitter and spit back gold. Gleaming
tintype of your portrait: tender

patina, hoarse laugh a winter
street's steaming, abraded velvet
whisper, heroin or chicken soup

slurped, a certain floating need
to make your bark your bite. One night,
in Dallas, you emptied your spit-

valve on my head as I tried to
shoot you from the lip of the stage.
Smiling, calling me names between

a solo's saddle and peak, you
rode us both the same way: letting
the notes you didn't play sing,

sing. Servant to old songs, and schools,
and to destroying them. Now we suffer
bankers in suits, with polished horns.

EVIDENCE OF BEAR

Like the dreamy housewife shrieking
Hitchcock shrieks at her refrigerator
repairman exposing himself in the kitchen
corner (he can't help it, he's been in hospital
recently) you imagine bear, sniffing your tent
deep in slanted night, under northern lights'
eelish dance, and you, psycho in your purple

bag of sleep. Haunches, hump, breath like bad
memories of a lover, invisible and steady,
his nose wrinkling muscle-twitch spasms
of nightmare in your calf. Grizzly will
investigate your grades, find them lacking.
Observe visits home to Mom have been
too infrequent. Shrug at your adjusted

gross income. But maybe he's her
and in a mood: salmon scarce, berries
not as ripe as wishes, cold wind spanking
her stupid cubs. Your leader's got a rifle,
but he's helpless in love or in Washington
lying to the voters. Your plan is fragile:
tell the bear how full of love for fur you are.

Kiss its footprint in the sand. Scat
with berries not so bad tasting really,
when your hunger claws. Think yourself
salmon, pink skinned, bloated but stealthy,
wiggling against the way things run, like
semen. Think about being born, silly baby,
into the big teeth of the planet.

THIRTY-THREE THOUSAND FEET

The burnt rusted wreckage of crumbling
hills fills canyons with the rub of time

and slant. The lightning-bolt switchback
trail climbs the naked face and on top

a giant polar bear rug of snow, legs
splayed, face buried in granite paws.

A volcano with labial caldera, frigid
and smokeless, hunkers down for the next

six hundred years. Cashmere clouds
graze the high desert, their shadows lazing

behind them on the rumpled ground.
Do parents own their children the way

clouds own their shadows? Do lovers?
The sun takes a spongy drink out of dimpled

whitecapped lakes, and offstage a relentless
can-crushing moon chugs the ocean tides.

In the pickled wastes of fallow farms,
in the pocked draws, pans and hollows

there are insects waving, clicking
"Have a Nice Day," their antennae provoking

every possibility. The failing light turns
trees to rose petal marmalade and the crimson

sky spreads a lead glass ceiling, waiting
for this earthquake fracture of feeling:

Dive in the river, even if it's dry.
Force pump the well, even if it's dry.

Despite the rig roads' suture of the cracking
mesa, despite the forest chopped for skiers'

speed, or blood on the tracks of the town
where you grew up—the little town you see

in every town you pass, quaintly stupid
and out of gas—you know this place rings pure.

That sunlight is a solution and the volcano's
for hire. That water always finds a way.

DARK CANYON: A BRIEF HISTORY OF THE RIVER

for Factor Grua

Does a river flow backwards like the blues
or blue memory of life as a child, kicking
out the rocks on every skinned-knee path
and lulling sleep on soft mother's lap?
Does the water conquer or divide? Is
there a sum of parts to swim? Whitewater
reveals only what it hides and dams stay dumb.

Every stone has a story it won't tell:
the cold truth of our own indifference
to what cannot be plundered or pursued.
A lake named Powell is like a bank named
Marx, the rapids now as still as the cool
glow of the television in Tucson
they've surrendered their lives to.

Yangtze or Penobscot, Bio-Bio
or Colorado, the same stream cannot
be drowned in twice. It moves wherever
you move, and you both move. Not just
in Lost Yak or Cataract, Tiger's Leap
or Lava, but inside the monotonous
crush of millennia, inside out.

The river is not there for you. If
you point and say, There is the river,
you lie. The river swims, with no mind
and all grace, out of the sun and into
the moon, swims over your rock bones, your
marrow of pool and drop, love and lack,
wet memory of fear and hope, and hope.

RAIN FOR NINETEEN HOURS

Delicious day of tent and rain, the wind
cold but not unloving, like mothers before
Spock. The silent torque of glacier, gentle
in its stones, goes at once both ways and stubs
its toe on bay. And when the sonic boom
of calving comes, dainty shavings of blue
bob and gurgle like synchronized swimmers.

Swimsuit models would not tolerate this
random havoc and scratch of snow. Sweater
supplies would stretch beyond redemption.
Rain in wild sheets like Klansmen riding swamps
knocks on my door in dream. Any salmon
in our net must be called a suicide.
Tonight, dinner will have the soggy warmth

of long goodbyes at airports. Goodbye. *Bye!*
I hear the faint whine of a distant plane
and with it goes the wilderness. Kiss. *Kiss.*
The sound of rain, like kitchen knives against
collarbones, makes danger out of dullness:
Fred Astaire tapping with an Uzi down
Main Street, or Sandman Sims, or Bojangles

on a steed. Nerves of men at altitude,
women in depression, lonely for themselves
but trapped with someone else, can't clear the sky
of tears or satellites blinking with regret.
This day is the day of distant mailmen,
cold, carrying on, asking themselves why,
while fat dogs lay low, growling dreams of meat.

THE SHADOWS OF KILIMANJARO

The tintinnabulation of the vegetation
in the plastic carcass of memory rings
like roadkill supper. The binge of clicking
heels frustrates birdsong's pleasure, but
a bushbuck's careful scatting—like Ella,
sober but still giggly girl-voiced, pushed
by Papa's mean ride and snare—educates
as it entertains the white man. This plant
smells like sage. This, like Lemon Pledge.
Bees cannot keep up with the demand

of the queen, buried in her mansion, bejeweled
with yummy throbbing torsos. The king
who's called a president—ivory staff
and infection at his side—bangs the mahogany
and beats enemies on the avenue named for him
and only him. A blow to the head
by the head of state, a blow to the crotch
by the crotch: such sweet irrupting
music of Nairobi makes hot days dance
the broken highlife shuffle of *who cares?*

SENDERO LUMINOSA

The slowness of graves in unburying
the dead is small thanks from earth for the way
it's been treated. Erosion is the bleak
thing between your legs and crooked river
banks will fail like all others. The tender
moon rises. The horse you ride tonight

explains the local news: mayor, teacher,
football coach, two women wearing glasses,
had their heads and feet sliced off by a crew
of comrades. The youngest of the killers
stayed behind to sew the heads and feet back
on, backwards: the feet, so they could not be
followed, the heads, so they could not be seen.
You're here to risk your life, but not reverse

the Conquest. These mountains hold no powder
as powerful as gun or coca leaf,
(the Incas' giddy revenge on white men)
but it's white mountains that brought you and will
deliver you whole. Bandits stick to trains,

but gravity can ruin your day on ice
sweating from the sun. The small boy who leads
your horse could be Tibetan, Navajo,
or mongrel, but is a campesino
named Jofino. In his rusted Cuzco,
Spanish is foreign, like war. Sendero
says, that will change soon. Not Spanish, but war.
Jofino's black eyes hold the reservoir
of hatred the war will fill. The darting

Urumbamba, damned for tourists, will run red.
Beggar on its gold throne, Peru will stand
and shout at sun. Metal detectors squelch
Pizarro's departure from Lima's airport.
Burial shrouds molt like snakes and snakes retake
the Amazon. A shining path, the truth.

Above you: gliding condors circle, pink
flesh of conquistadors in their glinting beaks.

CHINESE AIRSPACE

for Ethan Goldings

Impossibly still except for the bombing,
birdcalls and bombing, Tingri Plain rises
for another day where sun means butter.
A conclave of starlings whirls and bleats out
electronic game noise. Sniping
and mobbing, they circle above sheep
planning politics of hit and run. The Chinese
part of town is walled. The loudspeaker shouts
its message to the rest with the tinny garble
of all grand schemes. Good Morning Tibetans
we own your lives, the radio broadcast cackles
distorted and true. The try of local drivers
to accelerate their yaks over mountains
of indifference—Cho Oyo, Chomolungma,
the government—is not for show but tells:

they don't have a chance. Two skinny ponies,
barely stomping grain from chaff, spinning circles
over crumbling ground, are the singing tune.
Nowhere to go but around. Naked girls
wear spoons around their necks meaning nothing.
Truckers wear white gloves to better inspect
the customs they've run over. Crunched metal
on gravel running fake Buddha sculptures
from Kathmandu to Lhasa or runny-nosed
children reaching out for candy: pick your
prayer flag, name your choice. When mines are dug
and shells are shot, the charges buried into
hills will be sharper than skin or mind. The damage
done will be recorded at the better
universities and the birds won't care.

XANGMU

After landslides and three days' walk to town,
I get to play the Western stranger game:
a donkey eating cardboard on Main Street
and every other girl looks like a business.
Dogs growl when pinged with rocks, a stooped woman
sweeps the dirt street in front of her shop. Sweeps
the dirt from place to place, while down the block
fire cooks a truck cab cut from wheels, marooned.
The young women in doorways, picking lice
out of their boyfriends' hair, and the foul-mouthed
tiny boys firing their toy guns tell me
this would be a good place to die. Cheap, fast.

The fresh citrus stink of wet concrete competes
with shit. New buildings, brown walls already
cracking, bulge with cartons of Japanese
color TVs and booze from India.
Bent rebar tears the loose fabric of sky.
Sewage pipes run above and cross the street
leaking. Does a revolution smell like
this? While smoking men hold each other up
and drool, another tries to sell me knives
and money at rates too low to last. Signs
warn BEING CAREFUL OF FIRES AND ROBBERS.
Tonight, over the thump of the hotel's
karaoke, machine gun rounds echo
from the gorge of the Sun Kosi river.
Try before you buy. Eat what's on your plate.

This town is a mistake that opium
smuggled from Nepal cannot erase. Numb
in morning cold, I stand at the grated
border post waiting for the bribes, the stares,
the stamp of approval. I'm just passing
through like everybody else. I'm not here,
we're not there. A pack of small dogs crosses
the border. One yelps wildly when a boy
with a burned face grabs him by his front paws,
swings him around, smiles, and lets him hang.

THROW IT DOWN (WITH AUTHORITY)

for Mark Rowland & Jim Stern

Ernie Johnson in our studios will explain
the need for bonus coverage. Does TV enhance
the quality of our lives? The answer is

oblivious: of course. Planting a French
kiss on the muzzle of the Haitian Strongman's
gun will get you a version of sick we don't

have cures for. Yet. Crocodile rock. Beeper
boys in diapers troll for dirty cops, offering
sisters' mouths. Mary Maguire wins the convent

swearing contest each year, hands down. Kneepads
too. Fiddlesticks. Why, I'll be. Darn that dream
and bless it too, for without that dream I wouldn't

kung fu. A brick in mouth is better than two
at customs. Welcome to the Custerdome. Inside jobs
grin with cash. Genetic cruise control. Now this:

Never pass into the post until the man is ready.
Never break the dotted line on the break without
taking it all the way to the hole. Always throw it

down with authority. Never take it weak. Never
take it soft. Make your bed. Fight your father. Hit
back harder. Vote early and often. Use two hands.

YOUTHS ADRIFT IN A NEW GERMANY TURN TO NEO-NAZIS

is the headline fit to print hard by an ad
for Tiffany eighteen-karat Stars of David,
from hundreds cheap to thousands dear, depending

on the length of chain. Obermenzing, Allach,
Karlsfeld, Dachau, Walpertshofen, Rohrmoos:
the S2 subway gives all riders a choice

of stops. The violent ones are twelve,
thirteen years old. They don't remember
D-Day or B-29s. They don't remember fucking

Gorbachev. Are you shopping for news or
for jewelry? I can get you a deal. I can work
with you on this. Trust me. Like a fat SS

officer on a skateboard, a certain heaviness
of thought gathers momentum: if the spit polished
mark is the new jackboot, Benz can soft-shoe

a new factory in Alabama while the steel toe
kicks butt on worldwide currency markets
and baser metals of fear blacken Black

Forest skies. Motherland schmotherland,
it's no longer necessary to gain territory:
armies move in tanks and must be fed, money

moves in lightning fiber optic strikes,
feeding on itself. By modem, Claudia Schiffer
can breast-feed an entire nation of skinhead

bankers without removing her see-through
blouse, while Boris and Steffi entertain
their cooing housefrau moms. Don't tell me

ignorance is the cradle of distrust.
Don't tell me the Rockefeller Foundation
has funded a team of molecular biologists

to study whether Teutonic peoples sport
a genetic predisposition to *rude*. They're
searching even now for clues? Knocking

down the door to find the truth in its hiding
place, humping Anne Frank under the floorboards?
The truth gets around and won't take *No*

for an answer—even from a schoolgirl. Come
here my little Naziskins, my little mousefaced
cuddlemonkey, my skinpuppy lammykins. Listen

to the gurgle of the bedtime news: the ugly
beauty of arson, the reassuring snap of gypsy
bones dancing in unusual directions, birthday

celebrations for the greatest mustache
of them all. An ad for Siemens interrupts,
trumpeting systems integration technology:

Six Million Tons Of Steel A Year its slogan.
Cold rolled. On time. Highly adaptable
to customer needs. A new production record.

MONUMENT

The gross national product of Congo
is in a state of collapse, swooning
in the heat of tribal friction. Flagrant
fouls could be called at any juncture.
Tire changers in the pits work furious
for speed. Ballerinas court serious
injury while leaping off escalators
in toe shoes. They are Christmas shopping
for drugs to mute the pain of their leaping.
Shin splints, torn cruciates, stress
fractures. Let's follow these criminals
on their pas de deux perambulations. Stop

feeding at the Ben & Jerry's trough, cats
one to another, sucking in her ribs. In
the record store, a lone accountant considers:
Streisand or Midler? The choices we have
and take for granted while most of the world
suffers without. Concrete doubles asphalt's
price, Tylenol the generic's. A bluebird flies
into the plate glass windbreak. Now the jury
must consider: who manufactured the glass?
Who installed it? Who insured it? What role
did singular grains of sand play? Avaricious
dilettantes arabesque in search of answers.

Arbeit Macht Frei. Think about the market.
The trembling thick-tongued architect, truncated
by Parkinson's, references Midwest stockyards
and Rhineland kilns in his handsome iron-strapped
brick-towered museum. Out of the corner
of his monument, Jefferson winks. Yes, right
Bernard, I believe that was a wink we saw. Now
he's making his way to the South Lawn, waving
to the crowd. There's a thumbs up to the first
lady, who will stay in town to address the Breast
Cancer Conference tonight. He's on the chopper
steps now. A salute. One last wave. Back to you.

ISM

Driving out of town, fast but not too,
sharing a cockeyed joke and smoke, sniffing
the swag in the numbered box in the small
peace-loving snow-peaked banking kingdom,

then numbering victims with ballpark
estimates, so much plastique equals so
many spoony teens, truculent supervisors,
devils, devils, devils: sharp algebra

of extirpation. Now flip on the dinky
radio, and wait for the news at the bottom
of the hour: time, weather, local swill,
then, driving away still, the paroxysm:

the rebar separates from the concrete
the glass separates from the mullions
the skin separates from the bone
the mother separates from the son

no amount of money will fix it
no amount of campaigning will fix it
no amount of prison will fix it
no amount of mammaplasty will fix it

Wild screams, from the gut, then tears of
joy. Embraces, new cigarettes, still driving.
So much lucubration, so much knowledge gained
and love. Hours in cold rooms, concoctions.

Against such frippery as we declare, against
all palliative measures. Against the otiose
and the dumb. Some days are better than
others, but when ceiling finally kisses

floor, no day could be more cozy. Sleep
will come tonight, still driving, in black
coffee doses on the back seat, counting
victims jumping over fences, like sheep.

THE FACTORY

Ninety dollars an hour in Angola
Indiana will buy you lunch and more.
The factory has its needs, you have yours.
Renting yourself out to industry
is no big crime against family values.
True you are away from home. You are cold
beyond weather. But the man from Crooked Lake
writes the checks and all enjoy your presence.

From Plato, Mongo, and Brushy Prairie,
from as far away as Honeyville, men
come. And when they get the line up to speed
you hear the humming in their heads. Green, fast.
After love, work is the deepest thing you
give. This is both. When the hard winter sun
dies each day, money is your pillow. Night
turns your mind against itself. Sleep through it.

NOTHING ON TV (TONIGHT)

Someone named Bond paid 53.9 million dollars
for a painting by a guy who tried to shoot
himself in the heart and missed. Is that
desire or the collapse of desire? The yen

and the dollar are quite an item these days.
They are dancing in the center of the ballroom
and people that are being hired and people that
are being fired are bowing to their partners.

What love lies buried in ratings? What kind
of nursery rhyme is radiation and loneliness?
Is it too late to keep the banks safe from
lust? Are there gunmen in our mother's milk?

Quit asking questions, you tell yourself,
thinking of the luxuriant tank farms of
Jersey. Face facts. Madonna has more
body hair than you find appealing, and

yet her albums continue to sell. The
Lithuanian off-guard in Oakland goes to
the basket with the fervor of a capitalist
toady. The jumping frogs of the Ivory Coast

have sex in midair. Blue sweat is a blue-
green discoloration sometimes observed in the
sweat of copper workers. Humper's lump is an
affliction of lumber carriers that results in

the swelling of the lower neck. Disco digit
is a soreness or infection of the middle finger
caused by too much finger snapping while dancing.
Rectalgia is a pain in the ass, and mal de raquette

is pain caused by excessive use of snowshoes.
Irroration is the custom of watering a plant
with the discharge of a sick person to rid
the person (say, your aunt) of the disease

and give it to the plant. Strabotomy is the
surgical removal of a squint. Xysters are
bone scrapers and zomotherapy is treatment using
raw meat or the juices of same. Zipper trauma

is the term used by the *Journal of the American
Medical Association* to describe injury to the
penis from catching it in a zipper. The *British
Medical Journal*, on the other hand, prefers zip

injury. Guitar nipple refers to the irritation
of the breast that can occur from the pressure
of the guitar against the body. Gomphiasis
is a looseness of the teeth and graphospasm is

writer's cramp. Floccillation is the habit of
picking at one's sheets and blankets, as on a
deathbed, while carphology is a picking at one's
bedclothes. If you have a circumorbital

hematoma you have a black eye, and if you show
signs of mithridatism, you are immune to a poison,
by virtue of receiving over a protracted period
small doses of that poison, as with television.

GLOBAL UPSTREAM DIAPER DEVELOPMENT

Under thirteen stars and a pearly slice
of moon, the buttoned-down pink-skinned minions
of Cincinnati billabong tread

water at their desks for another day.
Happy shackles of good money and monster
benefits clink in the cafeteria

while ladies' smiles bloom in ads on soaps
for anti-rash and squeaking suds, dishes
smug with luster, shoulder snow condemned

to die in showery battles with the bottle.
Despite this kicking chorus line of clean,
all is never well or well enough: old

and unimproved, lives will end on darkest
dusty shelves, sclerotic and confused,
bitter being spurned by those once full

of raw desire. A goose can be cooked
in as many worthy ways as a cat skinned.
So someone has to venture out, to seek

and find another way, to waste not want
not around the infant middle. Gather,
maintain, offload goo. Hold pee for a price.

You took the charge and lived it well, flying
to Bangkok, Jakarta, Kuala Lumpur,
by rickshaw and longboat and tuk-tuk

you toured, by smoked glass taxi and bathtub
snorkeling you sweated, tethered to HQ
by the bilbo of E-mail and laptop,

calls home to the wife and sometimes kids, church
services in strange languages. Women
stuffed Luvs in factories blessed by Buddha,

pulp for Pampers thinned forests of their snaky
poisons. It's not a cure for cancer but
it's not cancer. You drunk free flying home.

BLUE ANGELS

Lateisha Terrell can't find the hundred dead
presidents to plea bargain her ten-year-old's
car stereo theft down to malicious mischief.
Welfare don't last till this time of month.
On Jefferson, the wrong angle of cap or tie
of laces will speed the aging process fast.
On Washington, you best be packing heat.
The pop pop of shootings in the breezeway
don't change weather or daddy's last visit.
It's not how long you make it, it's how you

make it long. Upside down, Blue Angels fly
above us, rattling windows in the stomachs
of the sunny bayside crowd. They crisscross
and loop, trailing smoke that keeps the empire
strong. Afterburners orange in climb, in dive
they scare seals but not tourists shopping
for souvenirs of this Fourth: American flag
ashtrays and *Death From Above* decals the steady
movers. When the plush cold of fog rumbles in,
the Angels loudly eat what's left of the sky.

THE WINTER GARDEN

Today on Broadway, we huddle from wind
beneath palms and piano fingers playing
Berlin: "God Bless America," slowly.
A man with socks for gloves and bags for shoes
applauds so sweet even guards with handguns
smile. "From way back," he says, "from way back when."
He's young. He doesn't know. He remembers
though something read in failing school, or dad's
tales of glory days before he left them:
the big war, dancehall widows wide with hope,
how cars cruised by with optimistic chrome.
Now a condo zoning-bonus is home.

The bored pianist plays "The Entertainer."
Another man, with beard of bus exhaust
and grease, shouts, "Hey, he's on the rag!" No one
gets the joke. He sorts his bottles, laughing
to himself. "Tell me the reason life smells
bad like socks," he says to no one, over
and over, his sockless ankles cracking
from the cold, the ragged flaps of sneakers
squeaking on the marble. The food stand sells
quiche and soup no one camping here can buy.
A sign says: *Winter Garden   This Is A*
Public Space   No Purchase Necessary

WITNESS PROTECTION PROGRAM

Food is the gun that plows the poor.
A fly on that boy's eye makes you sick.
Today's soy price firms a lovely hedge.

Deer can't swim in rising dam depths.
If you smash the head of a sheepdog
like a cantaloupe on a cable show,

the spray will stain your undershorts
at home through leaky copper coil.
Baby Bells snort with profits, mines reek.

When that man clobbered that woman,
when that car kissed that girl's face,
when those planes sprayed smart samples

into the sad camouflaged laps
of this month's weak sister, leaving
freeze-dried death masks, you changed

the channel. When body parts are tweaked
with pliers, redwoods drag behind claws,
or a dim student rapes his teacher

stars implode like anoxeric girls
who jump off the bridge of their desires
from heights the water slaps like sharks.

What father did to mother, or German
shepherd to the meaty leg of whitewashed
Negro, remains outside your jurisdiction.

I see a man in the park flying a kite—
making it spin like singing, slicing
the sky into pieces—from his wheelchair.

FRESH KILLS

In the chaos of phase space squats
the small sundog. See spot run. See
spot from comet's crash, parhelion
of curly ringlet in soft focus.

In the sloppy slopes of landfill,
forklifts ferry meals for gulls ripe
with hunger floating methane thermals.
Blue gas flames tease bellied children.

In the essence and presence of freesia,
nectarine or rose, a sniff of plucked
flower is scent but not true perfume.
In the lunar crush of days, refugees

cling to rotting timbers, carried
by currents past fragrant half-moon
beaches of well-oiled, drowsy tourists.
The living rank among the dead.